Forty-Six Views of Montlake Fill
by Constance Sidles and Hiroko Seki

First Edition

Copyright © 2014 Constancy Press, LLC

All rights reserved. No part of this book may be reproduced in any form or by any electronic or mechanical means, including information storage and retrieval systems, without permission in writing from Constancy Press, LLC.

All illustrations are used with permission of the artist, Hiroko Seki, who retains their copyrights.

Front Cover: Great Blue Heron
Back Cover: Mallards
Inside Back Cover: Photographs copyright © David Keller

Published and distributed by Constancy Press, LLC
Seattle WA 98105 USA

For additional copies of this book, write or call:

Constancy Press, LLC
4532 48th Avenue Northeast
Seattle WA 98105 USA
Phone: (206)522-7513
URL: http://www.constancypress.com

ISBN: 978-0-9842002-4-5 $34.95
Library of Congress Control Number: 2014914144

Printed in Hong Kong by Mantec Production Company
November 2014

Preface and Dedication

Two strangers met on the trails of Montlake Fill. One was a writer, essayist, and poet who came to the Fill nearly every day to observe birds in this oasis of nature set deep in the heart of a big city. The other was an artist, trained in Nihonga and Sumi-e, the ancient Japanese styles of painting. She had brought her sumi brushes and inks to the Fill to paint the nature she found here.

The artist showed her sketchbook to the writer. It was filled with images of all the things most beloved by the writer: tall cattails almost alive on the paper; swallows caught in mid-flight; wrens singing with heads thrown back; a turtle straining skywards; clouds pouring past Mount Rainier.

"These are beautiful," said the writer. Words began to swirl in her mind, poems to nature inspired by the wondrous beauty of the Fill, captured by the talent of the artist.

"I guess I am just crazy for painting," said the artist with a shy smile.

The writer cocked her head at this. "Crazy for painting," she repeated slowly. "That reminds me of the great Japanese woodblock artist, Hokusai. He called himself 'old man crazy for art.'"

The two women looked at each other. Their eyes shone. They recognized they were kindred spirits, connected by this magical place they both loved.

When she got home, the writer sent her poems about Montlake Fill to the artist. "What do you think?" she asked her new friend.

"You write like I paint," said the artist.

It was true. Both artists create their works by stripping away everything unnecessary, capturing the essence of nature—pure elegance that looks simple but is not.

"Let us do a book together," said the writer, "a tribute to the great Hokusai himself. He created 'Thirty-six Views of Mount Fuji,' then added ten more. Let us create forty-six views of the place we love best, Montlake Fill." The artist happily agreed.

You hold the results in your hands.

Dedication

To our husbands, John Sidles and David Keller, who have always believed in us and in our art

Table of Contents

	Page		Page
Winter		Spring	
Lifemates	3	True Beauty	26
Embers	5	Walt's Bench	29
Ice Dancing	6	Under the Bridge	30
Lazy Cormorants	8	He's So Fine	33
Old Man Rock	11	Blue-Collar Guy	35
Fog Brush	12	Curmudgeon at Heart	36
King of Diamonds	15	Young Love	39
Snowy Socks	17	Little Samurai	41
Winged Promise	19	Lost	42
Prelude	21	One and All	45
Snow Wings	22	Gossamer	47
		Hope	48
		Thief	50

Table of Contents (cont'd)

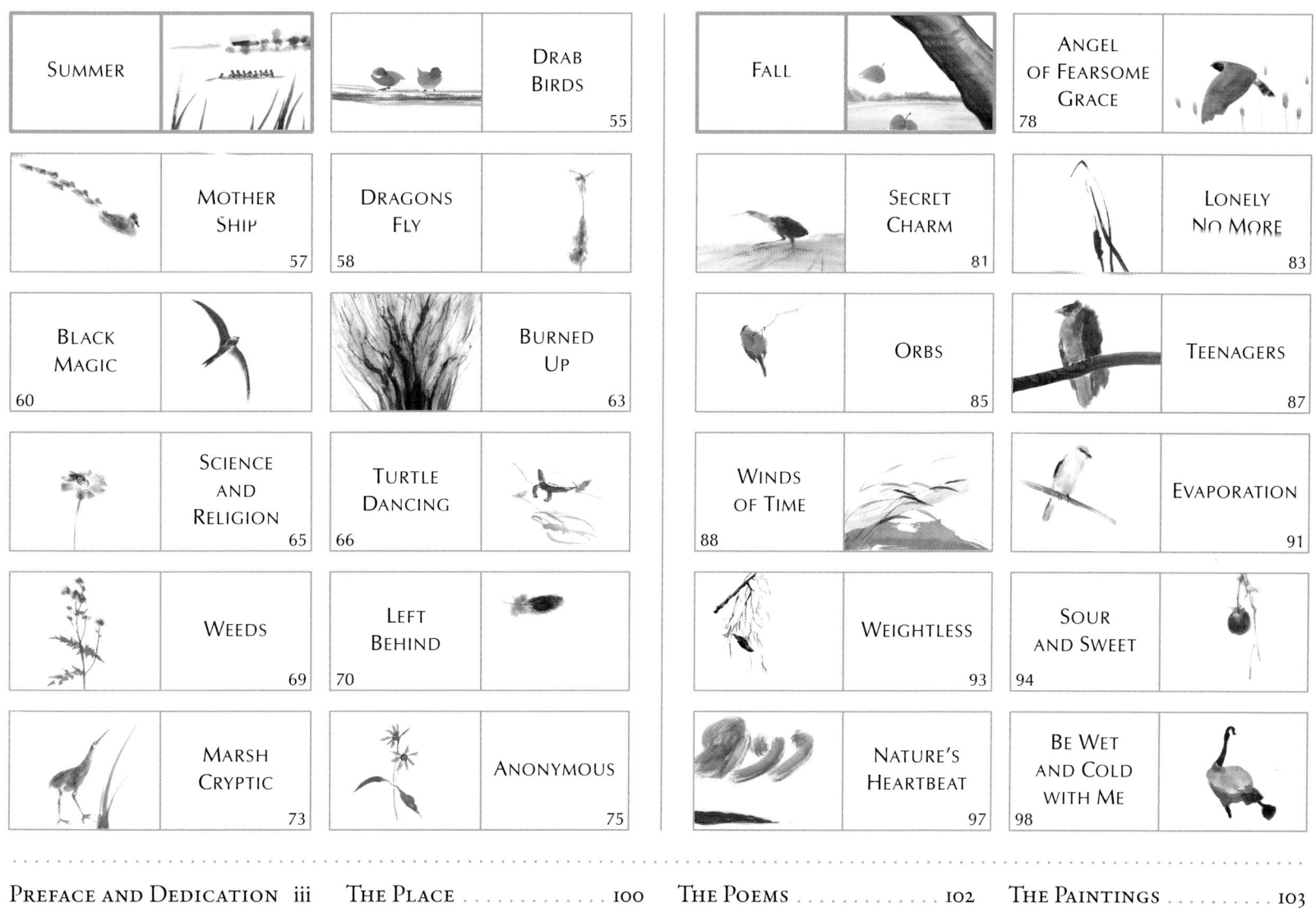

Summer	Drab Birds 55	Fall
Mother Ship 57	Dragons Fly 58	Secret Charm 81
Black Magic 60	Burned Up 63	Orbs 85
Science and Religion 65	Turtle Dancing 66	Winds of Time 88
Weeds 69	Left Behind 70	Weightless 93
Marsh Cryptic 73	Anonymous 75	Nature's Heartbeat 97

Angel of Fearsome Grace 78
Lonely No More 83
Teenagers 87
Evaporation 91
Sour and Sweet 94
Be Wet and Cold with Me 98

Preface and Dedication iii
The Place 100
The Poems 102
The Paintings 103
Index of First Lines . . . 104
Index of Paintings 105
Index of Species & Places 106

Winter

Today he leads.
Tomorrow he may follow:
a pair, mated for life.
But always they fly together,
soaring as one on widespread wings.

It must have been the howling wind
that fanned the ruby embers
of the kinglet's crown into flames
in the alder grove today,
warming me.

Cold.

So cold today.

Sky leaden.

Ground frozen.

On the lake

Trumpeter Swans,

floating like icebergs from the Arctic.

But alive.

So alive.

Down by the boathouse,
a poplar offers its branches
to sleepy cormorants.
Wake up, lazy birds!
It's time to fish!
I already drank my coffee.

Old Man Rock squats by the trail,
too stubborn to move,
speckled with guano.
The next rain will wash him,
and diminish him.

With fog-brush,
Nature paints a thousand grays:
pearl and ash, pewter, slate, charcoal...
and two gulls gliding
on glaucous wings.

The waters of Main Pond are muddy, opaque.
No matter.
The kingfisher dives and emerges
with a silver fish,
shedding drops of diamond.

Fog lifts its heavy skirts
from the land,
revealing the foot
of the mountain in the distance,
a giantess whose toes sport snowy socks.

In winter, one Barn Swallow ebbs and flows
in the ocean of air above the lagoon,
hunting insects on the fly.
A promise of spring to come.

Though trees may be bare,
stems brown,
Nature is not dead in winter.
It is furiously preparing.
Where do you think spring flowers come from?

Snow Geese honk high above the city.
Look up and you will see
their snowy wings,
dragging the last remnants of winter
behind them.

SPRING

She has neither education

nor money,

no conversation,

no waist even.

Drab, she blends into the background.

Her mate is enchanted.

So am I.

On Walt's bench,
you can watch the seasons turn,
from sleet to sun, heat to cold.
Walt, my friend, is gone now.
I sit here and find peace.

Under the bridge
where few can see
is a cathedral
carved by artist unknown.
For those who toil
love beauty
and take pride in creating it.

There is a reason
merganser males shine so brightly,
their ice cream-white heads a beacon
signaling to raptors:
I am here.
She requires it.

O blue-collar guy crazy for tools,
strong bill for fishing,
long plumes for flight.
Why are your soles clad in gold?
Must be for dancing.

In spring the Red-winged Blackbird
sings his cranky song in the marsh,
rough disharmony among the reeds.
I guess even grumps can be in love.

A young Tree Swallow
claimed the ramshackle nest box
no one else wanted.
It was all he could offer;
that, and himself.
She liked it.

The Marsh Wren, little samurai,
climbs up his cattail, prepared for battle.
He fights for his land and for his lady,
his only weapon a song.

Have you ever been lost in the wild
keening wind,
the rainbow just out of reach,
the slow beat of an eagle's wing?
I have.

We may all look alike,
act alike,
forage together,
flock as one.
But we each build our own nest,
create our own story.
Every life unique.

She used my hair and a spider's web
to weave her nest for two tiny eggs.
Spare of line, bare of color,
hidden from all prying eyes
but mine.

Can birds hope?
The grebe builds her nest each year,
unable to see the future
or tell if her chicks will survive.
Yet there she sits.

Thief in the night,
stealer of eggs,
stealer of lives.
How can you be so cute?

SUMMER

Now comes the time of obscurity,
when the migrants of spring
shed their bright plumage
and every songbird becomes dull.

In the pond,
a female Cinnamon Teal paddles with her babies,
mother ship followed by seven little tugboats,
fueled with green algae.

Dragons fly in summer at the Fill,
iridescent, opalescent
jewels to remind us that life
on Earth is ancient—
and still magical.

Black Swifts flew
down from their mountains today
to swirl above us,
sky-writing their secrets
with dark ink.
Soon the ink will disappear.

One hot July day,
arson-kids burned the Fill.
I saw it,
my beloved pine tree crowned with flame.
Dead now and black.
Food for woodpeckers.

Religion and faith ask:

How many angels can dance on the head of a pin?

Science and nature answer:

One bee at a time.

Maybe two.

Skyward soars
the swallows' wild dance.
A turtle strains
but cannot join.
Her elements are earth and water,
not fire or air.
Yet she dances.

We, the jury, find Thistle guilty.
You are a noxious weed!

Nature acquits.
Weeds are flowers too,
as beautiful as the hothouse rose.

Like a child's lost tooth,
the feather lies discarded,
unneeded now,
left behind by a bird
who grew new feathers
and flew away on the wind.

Shy bittern,
cryptic in the marsh,
tell me your secrets.
The bittern raises its bill,
sways like a fat reed,
and hopes I'll go away soon.

Fall

A Northern Harrier teetered over the lake,
coursing the reeds.
Angel of doom to its prey.
Seraph of ineffable grace to me.

Born of swamp and shade,
the Green Heron lives a secret life,
stalking solitude.
Seldom seen misanthrope,
you are beloved by us all.

The lonely cattails and wind sigh.
"We have no friend."
Soon swallows come
to play in the wind,
and a wren sings
from the cattail stalk.

Pale gold eyes for the girls,
dark ebon for males.
The universe is filled with orbs,
some the size of stars
others small but shining bright.

Cries fill the uncaring sky.
It is a young eagle calling his parents.
"Bring fish!"
They do not come.
He is old enough to catch his own now.

The winds of the Fill
caress the grass stems,
rustle the leaves,
blow the last dandelion seeds,
knock down trees.
Oh, sweet force of nature.

O nuthatch hanging from your tree,
nearly weightless
nearly free,
when you break the last bonds
of gravity and float away,
may I come too?

The last crab apple of fall
hangs lonely in the tree,
too wrinkled and sour to attract anyone.
It will feed the famished birds in winter.

I hear distant thunder of a coming storm,
the heartbeat of Nature.
A jogger runs by, ear buds playing rap.
Same planet, different worlds.

Heater is warm,
gravity heavy today.
It's hard to leave the house.
But the Fill calls:
Come and be wet and cold with me,
muddy—
and free.

The Place

Nature shapes the landscape relentlessly at Montlake Fill, helped sometimes by humanity's hand.

In the beginning, the Fill lay under an enormous ocean, far to the east of its present location. The land back then was concentrated into a single continent we call Pangaea. But 200 million years ago, the restless plates underneath that continent tore it apart, and the North American plate began to drift west, carrying our rudimentary continent on top. As it traveled, our continent collided with volcanic islands that had risen from the seafloor, and these islands were repeatedly welded onto our western shore. So the land grew until at last, the seafloor under the Olympics was pushed up in giant folds that joined the continent, and thus the land was complete. But not at rest; never at rest.

Two million years ago, our planet began to endure a series of Ice Ages, when glaciers from the north would advance and scour out deep valleys, retreat to the Arctic, wait a while, and inch back down again. Twenty thousand years ago, Montlake Fill lay under a glacier more than a mile thick. The glacier was a river of ice that blanketed the Puget Trough from the base of the Olympic Mountains to the upper reaches of the Cascade foothills. Nothing could live in such conditions, though the ice might have seemed a living thing, creeping inexorably over the land as it spread southward. The Fill must have been a lonely place then, the only sounds the crackling of the shifting ice and the quiet shush of the wind.

Eleven thousand years ago, the planet warmed and the ice melted, creating a vast lake. Montlake Fill became a muddy lakebed that hosted abundant freshwater shellfish, crustaceans, and insects, which in turn nourished large stocks of fish and huge flocks of birds. The air was now pierced by the clarion call of the loon and the whoosh of soaring swallows. Hairy mammoths, mastodons, and giant ground sloths roamed the mix of tundra and riparian lands nearby. Big though they were, the mammals were vulnerable and kept a wary eye out for long-toothed predators and even more dangerous bands of human hunters armed with sharp spears and arrows.

Conifer forests began growing where tundra and willow had reigned, and gradually, the nomadic hunters and gatherers who had lived in the open spaces gave way to tribes who were more settled, relying on the abundant salmon that migrated up the rivers and creeks that fed the lake. From time to time, foraging parties of Duwamish from the south would arrive at the lakeshore in canoes and harvest the mussels and fish that thrived in the clear waters of the lake. Women searched the surrounding forest of cedar and fir for edible bracken ferns and salmonberry, and men hunted for elk and deer. Occasionally they would leave behind artifacts of their presence: an arrowhead or two.

One hundred fifty years ago, white settlers began arriving in the region, and twenty years later, a few of them built their homes and businesses along the lakeshore. Among the biggest businesses was Henry Yesler's sawmill, a timber operation located in what is now Yesler Swamp, the easternmost boundary of the Fill. Yesler and other businessmen all around Lake Washington pressed the government to connect the lake to

The Place (cont'd)

Elliott Bay and the greater ocean so they could load their commodities onto ships and take them directly to market.

One hundred years ago, the U.S. Army Corps of Engineers agreed to connect the two bodies of water with a canal that cut through the narrow isthmus separating them. In 1916, the engineers opened the sluices of the Ballard Locks, and the lake emptied out into the sea, leaving a swath of mud behind for the University of Washington to own. Plants soon claimed the land, and it became marsh, swamp, bog, and ponds. In those days, such land was considered useless, so in 1921 when the City of Seattle offered to lease the site for a dump, the university was glad to agree.

For the next fifty years, garbage trucks and private vehicles brought their waste here and dumped it in. Gulls by the thousands and crows too came to feast on the bounty of our discarded trash. The methane generated by our garbage threatened to pollute the air, and burners were installed to burn off the gas. The furnaces roared day and night, long after the landfill finally closed.

Though the roaring flames are gone now, the methane still bubbles to the surface of the ponds, reminding us of what lies beneath. But above the layers of garbage, the land of the Fill has healed.

Now the grass of the prairies grows tall each year. The ponds give food and shelter to ducks, geese, and shorebirds. The rolling hills invite the swallows to swoop and the sparrows to sing. Swamps and marshes provide hiding places for shy waders and nesting sites for numerous species of birds: more than 200 different species of birds have been seen here since birders began keeping records in 1895. River otters breed in Union Bay on Foster Island to the south and come to the Fill to harvest mussels, eat fish, and sun themselves on an abandoned raft that floats offshore. Coyotes howl in tune with the firetrucks that occasionally wail past, and owls' eerie hooting haunts the night.

The trails that meander through the Fill take us humans away from the worries and hustle of the big city into a magical world that belongs to the wild things. Here, we connect to a deeper, slower part of ourselves, a part that hears the song of the wild in our hearts and is glad.

To celebrate the transformation of the land, we appended a new name to the Fill: Union Bay Natural Area. The name is proof that though we humans can sometimes lay waste to the Earth, our only home, we can also heal it.

Nature reclaimed, Nature restored and renewed. Wild again and full of life. Free.

The Poems

For many years, my kids have hounded me to join the twenty-first century. "You need to open a Facebook account," they say, "or LinkedIn. Start posting YouTube videos and Pinterest photos. Get a cellphone, for God's sake, and start texting. Nobody sends emails anymore, much less snail mail."

I've been reluctant because writing comes hard to me, and I didn't think I could fill the ravenous maw of social media day after relentless day. What could I possibly say each day that would merit the keystrokes? I might start out writing something worthwhile, and maybe I could keep that up for a week or two, but eventually I figured I would run out of originality. I would be reduced to writing about my mother's meatloaf recipe or some other trivia from my life. I would hate for people to think that the biggest event in my day was when I got the shower to start draining again.

"How about Twitter?" my persistent offspring asked. "Twitter is a microblogging service. Each text message is a maximum of 140 characters—including word spaces! You could write 140 characters every day, couldn't you?"

Yes, I thought, I could do that.

So I opened a Twitter account and discovered, to my dismay, that I would have to learn a whole new code to express myself. "The texts are almost incomprehensible," I told my kids. "There are so many symbols and abbreviations. I can't possibly learn a new language at my age, especially a high-tech one."

But my kids assured me I wouldn't have to. "Just write in ordinary sentences," they encouraged me.

So I began to write little posts about the nature I encounter every day at Montlake Fill, my favorite place on Earth.

I found my prose began to resemble spare poetry. Not haiku, because my verse is too free of structure. But Twitter's limits impose strictures as rigorous in their way as any form of short verse. I discovered that to say something original, meaningful, and lyrical with just 140 characters is wonderful discipline for a writer. It is the discipline of a new art form: Twitter poems.

Like the best sumi paintings, Twitter poems are stripped to the essential, the bare lines suggesting more than the eye can see. Twitter poems allow the senses to fill in the details from readers' own lives and thus connect us to each other, and back to Nature itself.

You can read all forty-six of the Twitter poems in this book in as many minutes. But I hope you will take your time with them instead, letting them connect you to Nature, letting Nature itself speak to you in the little quiet times, as the Fill so often speaks to me.—*Constance Sidles*

The Paintings

The symphony of nature begins when I set my dishes on the ground and hold a sumi brush in my hand.

On the stage are a Great Blue Heron, ducks, small birds flitting, geese, crows. In the middle of the orchestra, a Bald Eagle strikes his cymbals and the coots flock together in answer, running on the water's surface to join in. The orchestra members change suddenly like this with every breath of wind, every change of season.

As the conductor, innocently I paint, wrenching the movements of nature's creations out of my soul and onto the pages of my sketchbook. I paint moments in a flash of simplicity, as fast as the birds show themselves to me and then are gone, mere memories in my mind's eye but for a few strokes of my brush on paper. These are my sumi melodies in open concert.

Painting has been my muse since I was very young. When I grew a little older I began to paint in oils on canvas, longing for the look of European painters. Then a spirit welled up in me to return to my own heritage. I studied Nihonga, mineral pigments on byobu screens by apprenticeship, and worked at the Edo yuzen kimono facility painting freehand sumi on silk.

The simplicity of melodies I conduct comes from the confluence of "Studies" and "Heritage" with my own creative urge as I interact with nature. Can you sense my symphonic tones?—*Hiroko Seki*

Index of First Lines

A Northern Harrier teetered over the lake, 78
A young Tree Swallow claimed the ramshackle nest box, 39

Black Swifts flew down from their mountains today, 60
Born of swamp and shade, the Green Heron lives
    a secret life, 81

Can birds hope? The grebe builds her nest each year, 48
Cold. So cold today. Sky leaden. Ground frozen, 6
Cries fill the uncaring sky. It is a young eagle, 87

Down by the boathouse a poplar offers its branches, 8
Dragons fly in summer at the Fill, 58

Fog lifts its heavy skirts from the land, 17

Have you ever been lost in the wild keening wind, 42
Heater is warm, gravity heavy today, 98

I hear distant thunder of a coming storm, 97
If I knew the name of the flower, I would know its life, 75
In spring the Red-winged Blackbird sings his cranky song, 36
In the pond, a female Cinnamon Teal paddles with her
    babies, 57
In winter, one Barn Swallow ebbs and flows, 19
It must have been the howling wind, 5

Like a child's lost tooth, the feather lies discarded, 70

Misty gray Northern Shrike snagged like fog, 91

Now comes the time of obscurity, 55

O blue-collar guy crazy for tools, 35

O nuthatch hanging from your tree, nearly weightless, 93
Old Man Rock squats by the trail, 11
On Walt's bench, you can watch the seasons turn, 29
One hot July day, arson-kids burned the Fill, 63

Pale gold eyes for the girls, dark ebon for males, 85

Religion and faith ask: How many angels, 65

She has neither education nor money, 26
She used my hair and a spider's web to weave her nest, 47
Shy bittern, cryptic in the marsh, tell me your secrets, 73
Skyward soars the swallows' wild dance. A turtle strains but
    cannot join, 66
Snow Geese honk high above the city, 22

The last crab apple of fall hangs lonely, 94
The lonely cattails and wind sigh. "We have no friend", 83
The Marsh Wren, little samurai, climbs up his cattail, 41
The waters of Main Pond are muddy, opaque, 15
The winds of the Fill caress the grass stems, 88
There is a reason merganser males shine so brightly, 33
Thief in the night, stealer of eggs, stealer of lives, 50
Though trees may be bare, stems brown, 21
Today he leads. Tomorrow he may follow, 3

Under the bridge where few can see, 30

We may all look alike, act alike, forage together, 45
We, the jury, find Thistle guilty. You are a noxious weed, 69
With fog-brush, Nature paints a thousand grays, 12

Index of Paintings

Angel of Fearsome Grace (NORTHERN HARRIER), 79

Anonymous (ASTER SP), 74

Be Wet and Cold with Me (CANADA GOOSE), 99
Black Magic (BLACK SWIFT), 61
Blue-Collar Guy (GREAT BLUE HERON), 34
Burned Up (PONDEROSA PINE), 62

Curmudgeon at Heart (RED-WINGED BLACKBIRD), 37

Drab Birds (summertime's obscurity), 54
Dragons Fly (BLUE DASHER), 59

Embers (RUBY-CROWNED KINGLET), 4
Evaporation (NORTHERN SHRIKE), 90

Fall (falling leaf, COTTONWOOD SP), 77
Fog Brush (GLAUCOUS-WINGED GULLS), 13

Gossamer (ANNA'S HUMMINGBIRD), 46

He's So Fine (HOODED MERGANSERS), 32
Hope (PIED-BILLED GREBE), 49

Ice Dancing (TRUMPETER SWANS), 7

King of Diamonds (BELTED KINGFISHER), 14

Lazy Cormorants (DOUBLE-CRESTED CORMORANTS), 9
Left Behind (a discarded feather), 71
Lifemates (pair of CANADA GEESE), 2
Little Samurai (MARSH WREN), 40
Lonely No More (CATTAILS), 82
Lost (BALD EAGLE soaring), 43

Marsh Cryptic (AMERICAN BITTERN), 72

Mother Ship (CINNAMON TEALS), 56

Nature's Heartbeat (distant thunder), 96

Old Man Rock (too stubborn to move), 10
One and All (DARK-EYED JUNCO), 44
Orbs (BUSHTIT), 84

Prelude (COTTONWOOD SP in winter), 20

Science and Religion (HONEYBEE on CHICORY), 64
Secret Charm (GREEN HERON), 80
Snow Wings (SNOW GEESE), 23
Snowy Socks (Mount Rainier), 16
Sour and Sweet (PACIFIC CRAB APPLE), 95
Spring (YELLOW FLAG IRIS in the rain), 25
Summer (rowers on Union Bay), 53

Teenagers (juvenile BALD EAGLE), 86
Thief (RACCOON), 51
True Beauty (female MALLARD), 27
Turtle Dancing (RED-EARED SLIDER), 67

Under the Bridge (Montlake Bridge), 31

Walt's Bench (seasons turning), 28
Weeds (CANADA THISTLE), 68
Weightless (RED-BREASTED NUTHATCH), 92
Winds of Time (blowing grass stems), 89
Winged Promise (BARN SWALLOW), 18
Winter (Wooden Bridge with winter snow), 1

Young Love (TREE SWALLOWS), 38